Living and Nonliving

Revised and Updated

Angela Royston

Heinemann Library
Chicago, Illinois

Customer Service 888-454-2279
Visit our website at www.heinemannlibrary.com

Editorial: Diyan Leake
Design: Joanna Hinton-Malivoire
Picture research: Melissa Allison and Mica Brancic
Production: Duncan Gilbert

Originated by Chroma Graphics (Overseas) Pte Ltd
Printed and bound in China by South China Printing Co. Ltd
12 11 10 09
10 9 8 7 6 5 4 3 2

Library of Congress Cataloging-in-Publication Data
Royston, Angela.
 Living and non-living / Angela Royston– New ed. –
  p. cm – (My World of Science)
Includes bibliographical references and index.
   ISBN 13: 978-1-4329-1446-2 (HC)   ISBN 13: 978-1-4329-1468-4 (Pbk)
   ISBN 10: 1-4329-1446-4 (HC)   ISBN 10: 1-4329-1468-5 (Pbk)
1. Life (Biology)– Juvenile literature. [1. Life (Biology) 2. Death.] I. Title.
  QH325 . R69 2003
  570--dc21
                        2002009402

Acknowledgements
The publishers would like to thank the following for permission to reproduce photographs: © Bruce Coleman Collection pp. **5**, **22**; © Chris Honeywell pp. **15**, **26**; © David C. Tomlinson p. **13**; © Digital Vision pp. **10**, **19**, **25**; © Getty Images p. **18**; © KPT Power Photos p. **11**; © NHPA p. **24**; © Photodisc p. **7**; © Pictor International p. **20**; © Powerstock Zefa pp. **4**, **16**; © Robert Harding Picture Library pp. **12**, **17**; © Trevor Clifford pp. **8**, **9**, **14**, **23**, **27**, **29**; © Trip pp. **21** (H. Rogers), **28** (G. Contorakes); © Wildlife Matters p. **6**.

Cover photograph reproduced with permission of
© Masterfile (Ledingham/Boden).

The publishers would like to thank Jon Bliss for his assistance in the preparation of this book.

Contents

Any words appearing in the text in bold, **like this**, are explained in the glossary.

What Is Living?

This cat is living. You can tell that the cat is alive because it is licking its paw. If there is a loud noise, it will jump.

Elephants and people are animals. All animals are living things. There are many different kinds of living things.

Plants

These plants are alive and growing. You can tell they are alive because they have green leaves. Each plant grows from a **seed**.

Trees can go on growing for many years. Each year they grow new twigs, branches, and leaves. Some trees grow flowers every year.

What Is Nonliving?

None of the things in this picture are living. They cannot move on their own. They will only move if they are pushed.

This doll cannot move and it does not grow. Nonliving things stay the same unless something else changes them.

Moving

These zebras are **galloping**. Animals can move by themselves. Most animals have legs, wings, or **fins**. They use them to move.

Nonliving things cannot move on their own. A car or truck can move very fast, but a person has to start the **engine** and then drive it.

Senses

Animals and people can see, hear, feel, smell, and taste. This is how they know what is going on around them. Seeing, hearing, feeling, smelling, and tasting are called **senses**.

Plants have different senses. Their senses allow them to **react** to the world around them. A sunflower grows upwards. The flower turns so that it always faces the Sun.

Eating and Drinking

Living things need to eat food and drink water to stay alive. What is in the sandwich that this boy is eating? (Answer on page 31.)

Plants use their leaves to make their own food. They take in water through their **roots**. Plants die if they do not get enough water.

Finding Food

cheetah

antelope

This cheetah is hunting an antelope. Some animals, like the cheetah, eat only meat. Others, like the antelope, eat only plants.

Nonliving things do not eat and drink. This lion is carved out of stone and so it is nonliving. Even if you put food in its mouth, the lion will not eat it.

Breathing

Living things need to take in **oxygen**.
Oxygen is a type of **gas**. Humans
breathe in oxygen from the air.

Fish take in oxygen from water.

Snails and plants take in oxygen, too. Plants give out oxygen at night. But rocks do not breathe. Nonliving things do not need oxygen.

Getting Rid of Waste

All living things **produce** waste. The brown cowpats are waste from the two cows. **Urine** is also waste that animals get rid of.

This statue is covered with waste. The statue does not produce waste because it is not alive. Which animals have produced this waste? (Answer on page 31.)

New Life

Living things **produce** babies or **seeds** that will grow to become like themselves. These puppies will grow up to be adult dogs like their mother and father.

If these seeds are planted, they will grow into new plants. But spoons will not make copies of themselves. This is because they are nonliving.

Living Things Die

Many flowers and **insects** live only for a few months. Then they die. After they have died, they slowly **rot** away.

Some living things live for just a few years. Others live for many years. A giant tortoise could live for 100 years before it dies.

Things That Were Alive

These things are made of wood. Wood comes from trees that were once alive. Wool, paper, and cotton also come from things that were once alive.

Things that were once alive have to be **treated** to stop them from **rotting**. Nonliving things do not rot.

Plastic toys do not need to be treated to stop them from rotting.

Living or Nonliving?

The children, the puppies, and the flowers are living things. Which things in the picture are nonliving? (Answer on page 31.)

The table, the sofa, and the door are nonliving. There are four living things in this room. What are they? (Answer on page 31.)

Glossary

breathe pull air or oxygen into the body, then push it out

engine a machine that makes something move

fins flat parts of the body of fish and other water animals. The animals use their fins to steer.

gallop run fast with all four feet off the ground at the same time

gas something that has no shape. It spreads out through the air.

insect small animal with six legs and feelers called antennae. Bees, flies, ladybirds, and beetles are all insects.

oxygen a kind of gas that all living things need to breathe

produce make

react do something as a result of something else happening

roots the parts of a plant that are below ground

rot slowly break up into little pieces

seed part of a plant that grows into a new plant

senses the ways in which a living thing finds out about what is around it. Seeing and feeling are senses.

treat protect something using special chemicals

urine liquid that animals make to get rid of unwanted water

Answers

Page 14—The sandwich contains lettuce, cheese, tomato, ham, and cucumber.

Page 21—The birds have produced the waste on the statue.

Page 28—The fence, the basket, and the children's clothes are nonliving.

Page 29—The girl, the dog, and the two plants are living

More books to read

Ganeri, Anita. *How Living Things Grow: From Seed to Sunflower.* Chicago: Heinemann Library, 2006.

Mayer, Cassie. *Living and Nonliving: Ocean.* Chicago: Heinemann Library, 2007.

Mayer, Cassie. *Living and Nonliving: Rainforest.* Chicago: Heinemann Library, 2007.

Index